W9-DIB-511

DRUGS AND THE MEDIA

Television and other media are powerful influences in our lives.

DRUGS AND THE MEDIA

Mary Price Lee
Richard S. Lee

THE ROSEN PUBLISHING GROUP, INC.
NEW YORK

To Ginny and John Purinton
in friendship, and all that jazz.

*The people pictured in this book are only models; they in no
way practice or endorse the activities illustrated. Captions
serve only to explain the subjects of the photographs and do
not imply a connection between real-life models and the
staged situations shown. News agency photographs are
exceptions.*

Published in 1994 by The Rosen Publishing Group, Inc.
29 East 21st Street, New York, NY 10010

First Edition

Manufactured in the United States of America

3 9082 05709366 1

Library of Congress Cataloging-in-Publication Data

Lee, Richard S. (Richard Sandoval), 1927-
    Drugs and the media / by Richard S. Lee and Mary Price
    Lee.
    p.   cm.—(The Drug abuse prevention library)
    Includes bibliographical references and index.
      ISBN 0-8239-1537-9
      1. Drugs and mass media—United States—Juve-
      nile literature. 2. Substance abuse—United
      States—Juvenile literature. I. Lee, Mary Price.
      II. Title. III. Series.
      HV5825.L434 1993
      070.4'4936229'0973—dc20   93-21099
                                  CIP
                                    AC

Contents

Introduction

*D*rugs are all around you. Some, like crack and marijuana, are illegal but easy to buy on the street. Others, like liquor, wine, beer, and cigarettes, are legal. They can be purchased in stores if you're old enough, and sometimes even if you're not.

We have an attitude in this country that makes it seem cool, glamorous, and fun to use legal drugs. Advertisements almost always show liquor and cigarettes being used in fun situations. One of TV's longest-running, highest-rated sitcoms takes place in a bar. Tobacco companies, no longer allowed to advertise on TV, instead sponsor TV sports events.

This same attitude carries over into illegal drugs. Drug dealers are portrayed in movies and TV shows and even in newspapers and magazines as rich dudes with gold jewelry and big cars. Yet when a drug dealer is picked up by the police, not much is said because our court system first has to *prove* that the person dealt drugs. And when there's a big drug bust, all we see on

TV are the guns and money taken by the police, and the clever dodges used to hide the drugs. We rarely find out what happened to the so-called dealers.

Drugs have always been around, but they have become easy to get and glamorous only in the last 30 years. What is called "the drug culture"—the idea that anything you want to do, including drugs, is okay—started with drug use by rock musicians and other celebrities in the 1960s. It spread to the lower classes—the poor in ghettos and slums—as a way to escape grinding poverty and lack of hope. It also spread to teenagers wanting to rebel against their parents and "do their own thing." It has never stopped.

The "media" is a term that stands for every kind of message, advertisement, and entertainment that reaches us. The drug-related events of the 1960s were news. Drugs are still news. Only now, some people are coming out in the media and saying, "Hey, drugs are wrong!" That trend is welcome.

This book will show how the media can trick you into believing it's okay to smoke, drink, even do illegal drugs. But first, we'll show you how you can get talked into trying drugs, and why drugs are a bad idea.

Friends share a lot of things, but the decision to do drugs is your own responsibility.

CHAPTER 1

What's Your Decision?

Jan met Beth after school. Although they were friends, Jan thought Beth had been cool to her lately, and that hurt. The way she felt about herself, Jan needed all the friends she could get. But today, Beth approached with a smile.

"Hi, Jan, what's happening?" Beth asked.

"Not much," Jan replied. "My mom's working day shift from now till forever, so I'm stuck with the housework. It's a pain in the butt. Someday I'll get even!"

"Why go home?" Beth said. "Lateef's got some Colombian grass out at the hideout. A bunch of us are going. Come on!"

Jan wasn't sure. She thought Beth smoked pot, but this was the first time she'd

10 *been asked to share. Jan had heard that marijuana wasn't really "doing drugs," but was just a way of getting away from problems for a while. And Jan had problems! She wanted to be part of the group. She had an idea trying pot would be fun. She'd seen people smoking it at the rock concert last summer, and nobody had gotten rowdy. Grown people smoked and drank, and that was okay.*

Jan was tempted. And yet...

Why Some Teenagers Do Drugs

Maybe you've been invited to do drugs like Jan. Maybe you've already tried some. Jan's story shows you lots of reasons why it's tempting to say yes. Here they are again:

"The way she felt about herself, Jan needed all the friends she could get." It's natural to want people to like you, especially if you don't feel too hot about yourself.

"Someday I'll get even!" If you're angry with someone at home, doing drugs can be a form of revenge.

"A bunch of us are going." and **"She wanted to be part of the group."** It feels good to be "in." People your age are your *peers*, and they can exert pressure

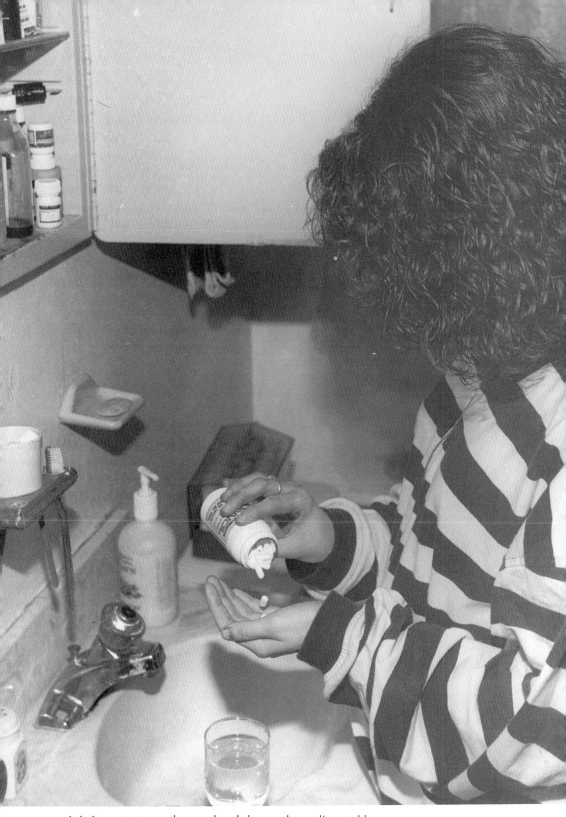

It is important to take any legal drug only as directed by your doctor or as the packaging label specifies.

16 lead to cross-addiction with alcohol. *All* addicts find it very hard to get clean. Not too many manage it.

The Different Kinds of Drugs

Illegal or "street" drugs include:

Uppers. These stimulants increase your heart rate and blood pressure. The *caffeine* in soft drinks, coffee, and tea is a very mild upper. *Marijuana* (also called "pot" and "grass") is an upper made from the *Cannabis sativa* plant. Among the 400 chemicals in pot smoke is *tetrahydrocannabinol* or THC. It boosts the heart rate and causes reactions such as sensitivity to light and sound, loss of control of muscle movement, and sometimes unpleasant mood changes. It takes up to a month for your body to get rid of the THC toxins. The amount of THC in the marijuana sold has more than doubled in recent years. Pot is more cancer-causing than tobacco. If used a lot, it can affect your memory and make you lose interest in life.

The most powerful upper is *cocaine,* made from the leaves of the coca plant. Cocaine is expensive. Its very hefty kick delivers a false sense of strength. You feel a short rush of activity followed by a sudden crash. Cocaine can be sniffed as a powder, injected as a liquid, or smoked as crack. (Remember that unclean needles are a major source of infection with HIV, the virus that causes AIDS.) Cocaine is highly addictive, and *crack* is its most addictive form. Cocaine can cause a stroke. An overdose can kill you, often by speeding up the heart and causing a heart attack.

Some prescription drugs are dangerous uppers, especially if overdosed. One is *methamphetamine*, called "speed" or "meth."

Downers. These drugs slow your body's reactions and cause a retreat from reality. *Barbiturates*, usually used as sleeping pills and relaxers, are very dangerous downers. An overdose can kill.

Narcotics. These are designed to relieve pain, like morphine, but they are also misused in the form of *opium* and, most often, *heroin* (also known as "junk," "horse," and "smack"). All are made from the poppy plant. The effect, especially of injected heroin, is a powerful, relaxing high that lasts up to six hours. During the high, the body craves more heroin, and users often overdose. The high is followed by a heavy, painful downer that can last for days. Heroin is the most habit-forming

For some, even social drinking is not appealing.

of the street drugs. It is very expensive. **19**
The body quickly demands more and more
heroin to overcome the long downer, and
to repeat the high. This cycle is impossible to stop without medical help.

Hallucinogens. These are a class of
drugs that includes *LSD* ("acid") and *PCP*
("angel dust"). They can make you see
things that are not there and believe you
can do the impossible. Some trips with
these drugs end in death.

Legal drugs include:

Alcohol. The leading drug problem for
young people is alcohol. It is easy to get,
often addictive, and can be very toxic.
Even one drink makes some people ill.

Alcohol is a downer. The sugar in a
drink may seem to deliver a small spurt of
energy. But the ethyl alcohol in any drink
from beer to brandy is dangerous. It may
cause relaxation at first, but later mood
changes, forgetfulness, clumsiness, inabil-
ity to speak or see clearly, and possibly
unconsciousness.

Many people your age, and many
adults, do not consider drinking beer to be
"drinking." But there is the *same amount
of alcohol* in a 12-ounce bottle or can of
beer as in a 1 1/2-ounce drink of hard liquor or a 5-ounce glass of wine. The

20 average person can throw off the effects of alcohol only at the rate of one drink an hour. So it is easy to take too many drinks, and it takes a long time to recover. Black coffee and fresh air will *not* make you sober. Time is the only cure for the "hangover" that follows, with its headache, tiredness, and feelings of sadness. About 10 percent of people who drink alcohol become alcoholics; that is, they become addicted to the point where getting alcohol to drink becomes the most important thing in their lives.

Tobacco. Years ago, nearly half the people in this country smoked—mostly cigarettes. Now, only about 25 percent of Americans are smokers. But still, there are one million new young smokers every year, and over 100,000 are under age 13.

Why? Because people your age see adults smoking. You don't see anything bad happening to them. You think it's cool to light up and hang out, away from parents, nerds, and dweebs. You've seen adults glare at you for smoking, and you may think *that's* cool. But smoking is *not* cool. It is very dangerous.

Tobacco use becomes a habit faster than any other drug, and the earlier someone starts, the harder it is to stop.

Advertising often suggests that smoking and drinking go hand-in-
hand with youth, success, and a good time.

22 *Nicotine* in tobacco smoke can hook you almost immediately. Once your body has had it, it demands more. Nicotine speeds up your pulse, yet reduces the blood that reaches your heart. Cigarette smoke also contains *carbon monoxide*, the same killer gas that comes from auto exhausts. The sticky brown *tar* in tobacco smoke causes many kinds of cancer and other serious diseases. It may take years of smoking for these diseases to appear. That is why most smokers deny the danger—and why the tobacco industry will not admit the danger exists. Because a dependence on nicotine is one of the hardest to break, thousands of people who truly want to quit find they cannot.

Doctors have proved the connection between smoking and disease many times. There is no longer any doubt. It is a fact that 10 times as many smokers die of lung cancer as nonsmokers do. Even nonsmokers who live with smokers are more likely than other people to develop smoking-related diseases.

Some of the media tell you these bad things about drugs, smoking, and drinking some of the time. But more effort is made to get you to drink and smoke. Let's talk about that next.

CHAPTER 3

What Are "The Media"?

*T*he *media* are sources that tell or show you things (TV and radio news, newspapers, magazines). The media may also try to change how you think about things (talk-show hosts and guests, radio personalities, and DJs). The main support of the media is *advertising*. If you include all forms of advertising as part of the media, "the media" become far broader. They now include direct mail, store displays, billboards, and sponsorship of sporting and music events. They also include ads on radio and TV and in magazines and newspapers.

Consumers of all ages make choices based on the "sights and sounds" of repeated advertising.

We include *entertainment* as part of the media. Most of what you see or hear on the electronic media—TV and radio—is pure entertainment. Every celebrity, from politician to punk rocker, depends on the media for his or her fame. Also, every form of public entertainment, from a rock concert to a movie, absolutely depends on the media for advertising. And TV and radio entertainment happens because advertisers pay for the air time.

You are surrounded by the media. If you see a hip-hop movie, watch music videos on MTV, or buy a rock CD, you are receiving information or entertainment from the media. If you read a newspaper, you are getting news, opinions, and advertising. The trick to managing the media is *to see the messages for what they want you to do.* Some messages are pure information, but others are meant to persuade you to buy products. Often, advertising goes beyond reality (camels playing pool) to get your attention.

Your best defense against media influence is to ask yourself, "Do I really need or want this?" and "Do I really believe this, or want to do this?"

CHAPTER 4

How Does Advertising Persuade?

*D*ifferent forms of media work together to influence you. You watch a rap group on MTV or elsewhere on TV. That's entertainment. The name of their latest CD is mentioned on the show. That's *influence* mixed with the entertainment. You decide you want the CD. You find it advertised in the newspaper, and you see a big display at the record store. This is an *advertising campaign:* The TV or radio message, the newspaper ad, and the store display are all working together.

That is how things are sold, from soft drinks to shoes, from airline tickets to automobiles. Most marketers use many steps to get you interested in a product. They make it easy to find and to buy. Is anything wrong with that?

Billboards are part of the landscape. That kind of advertising is visible to everyone.

28 | *The "Twist" Is Not a Dance!*

What *is* wrong is the "twist" that some advertisers put on their products. It's not the old-time dance made famous by Chubby Checker. It is the tricks advertisers use to make a product look attractive. This glamorizing is a form of peer pressure. Ads—especially TV ads—use color and movement to make the product seem a part of being successful, popular, or one of the group (athletic shoes). Other ads make the product a part of having fun (beer). *The pressure comes if you think you must buy certain products to be popular, successful, or happy.*

Why do auto ads show cars going fast? Why do beer ads show people partying? Why do cigarette ads show more than one person in a fun setting? Why do cigarette ads aimed at women show ultrathin women? Why is there a "you-need-it" message in ads for athletic shoes? Why do celebrities advertise everything from shoes to soft drinks? The basic message behind every ad is: "Buy me!" It's all done to make people believe that these products will somehow make them happy, admired, or attractive. When people believe that a product can improve their lives, demand for the product increases.

Are Advertisers Targeting Teenagers? 29

Drug dealers are probably the only marketers in the world who can sell their products without advertising. When it comes to the *legal* drugs alcohol and tobacco, advertisers spend plenty. Tobacco companies spend over $327 *billion* a year in advertising—almost $10 million a day! And some of that advertising is targeted at you, even though you're too young to smoke. Advertisers deny that they're reaching out for you. But...

Why else would cigarette companies see that their ads and coupon offers get into

Teenagers are important consumers. A lot of money is used to advertise products that may be of interest to them.

30 magazines you read? Why else would Old Joe Camel be shooting pool on a billboard dominating the boardwalk at a resort where thousands of teens go every June to celebrate Senior Week? Why would the Marlboro Man look cool in magazines and on billboards? Why would cigarette brand names appear on racing cars?

Advertisers are counting on these messages to get you to do what *they* want. Magazine offers of Joe Camel jackets and caps promise to make you look like part of the crowd, and grown-up, too. Billboards at places where you gather with friends say it's cool to smoke. The effect of advertising is just as much pressure on you as the peer pressure that may make you light up or drink up even if you don't want to.

This whole idea is called "brand awareness" by advertisers. The more places you see the name of the product—especially if it's associated with fun, popularity, or success—the better the chance that you'll try it sometime. Advertisers would like you to buy now, but they don't mind waiting.

Afternoon Scene

"I know where we can get cigarettes," said Alex as he and Jerome were leaving school. "At the convenience store."

"Naah," said Jerome. "You gotta be eighteen. They'll know you're not."

"Big deal! They sell 'em to me, anyway. They sort of look around to see if anybody's watching, but what cop's going to bother them? And they're making money."

"Well, you go in," said Jerome. "But if you can get one of those fancy boxes of six packs, we'll split them and send off the coupon for stuff, too."

"Okay, but you're weird, Jerome! You send me in for the smokes, but you lie when you fill out the coupon that asks if you're eighteen."

"Who's to know?"

Alex headed for the store as Jerome waited. In a few minutes, he returned, tossing the package into the air. "No problem," he said. "The lady says, 'Are you eighteen?' I say, 'Yeah.' She looks at me funny, but she takes my money."

"Maybe I could have gotten them after all," Jerome said.

"You could have, I guess. Those special packs are down low, under the counter. Even a nine-year-old could reach them," Alex said.

"Hey, a nine-year-old wouldn't care."

Jerome is right. A nine-year-old might not try to smoke, but wait three or four

There are many ways to have fun with friends without drinking or doing drugs.

years! Kids as young as 12 are smoking. Here are some heavy numbers:

- One-third of all teens do some smoking by age 18. And 90 percent of those will start smoking before age 21.
- Nearly 30 percent of all high school seniors smoke.
- Tobacco companies want 5,600 new smokers a day to make up for people who quit (or who die)! They are close: About 3,000 teenagers and preteens start smoking each day. These new young smokers buy *947 million packs* of cigarettes a year.

Do Tobacco Ads Affect People Your Age?

The Centers for Disease Control says that young people *are* influenced by cigarette ads. Their survey of 1,396 teenagers found that most smokers aged 12 to 18 prefer the three most heavily promoted brands. Some 69 percent smoke Marlboro, a brand with a macho campaign that uses the outdoors to show independence and strength.

The third-ranking brand in the survey is promoted by Old Joe Camel and his animal friends. In another survey, Joe Camel was recognized by children aged three to six almost as easily as Mickey Mouse!

34   Cigarette advertising is placed in magazines and newspapers. Here are some interesting recent estimates from a national study. It covered "demographics," a fancy word for the study of the numbers and ages of people. The estimates cover three of the many publications that accept cigarette advertising:

- *Motor Trend*, a popular magazine, is seen by over 4.5 million people. About 1.2 million, or almost one quarter of them, are aged 12 to 17, legally unable to buy cigarettes.
- *People* is seen by more than 30 million Americans. An estimated 6.5 million, or one out of every five who see the magazine, are aged 12 to 17.
- *Rolling Stone,* an entertainment publication that also carries liquor ads, is seen by 7.5 million people. One out of five is aged 12 to 17.

These young people are not subscribers and may not read the publications mentioned. But they are exposed to them, and advertisers know that they glance at the pictures and the ads.

Do Magazines Report the Dangers?

Yes, they do. However, those that rely heavily on cigarette ads for their income are far less likely to write about the dangers of smoking. That is the finding of a 25-year review of 99 magazines by *The New England Journal of Medicine*. Magazines with tobacco ads were 38 percent less likely to cover smoking risks than those with no tobacco ads. Women's magazines with cigarette ads were 50 percent less likely to run antismoking articles. And as cigarette ads went up, articles against smoking went down.

The media don't care whether you get hooked on smoking, so *you* have to care, and outsmart them. Look at their come-ons as ways to get you into trouble.

Whole Lot of Partying Goin' On!

Television and other ads for liquor and wine sell a cool life-style as much as they sell products. Beer ads are different. From the "party animal" to the Swedish bikini team, most beer ads have several things in common:

- They show people in groups. The not-so-secret message: You don't belong if you don't drink beer.
- These people are having fun, comparing beers, and having beach parties. The message: You won't enjoy yourself if you don't drink beer.

36

- In ads, beer-drinking is often associated with the outdoors and recreation. The message of these ads is: You have to drink beer to enjoy sports and recreation fully.
- The fact that beer contains alcohol is never mentioned. Even the few ads that mention responsible drinking (as in knowing when to say *when*) don't mention any downside or ill effects. There are no health warnings in beer or liquor ads.

There is no truth in any of these ideas! You do not need to drink to be part of a group. Your group does not need to drink beer to have fun. There's no outdoor activity, from jogging to softball, that anyone ever played better after several beers. Yet people of all ages seem to accept the message about drinking outdoors. The Office of the U.S. Surgeon General says that 41 percent of drowning deaths and 60 percent of boat-related drownings are alcohol-related.

The liquor industry, like the tobacco industry, sells fantasy instead of reality. And it spends nearly $2 *billion* a year doing it. More than $675 million is spent by beer companies alone, mostly for TV advertising during sports events.

Many schools and communities have programs to educate young students about the dangers of drugs.

It is estimated that by the time you reach 21—now the legal drinking age all over the country—you will have seen 100,000 beer commercials. And you will have seen the many beer and cigarette bill-boards that the cameras pick up as they follow the action in the sports stadiums.

38 | *The Billboards That Roar*

An auto-racing trophy is named after a cigarette brand. Other tobacco companies sponsor auto-racing teams, so the name of the cigarette appears on TV every time the cars circle the track. Cigarette companies also add their support—and brand names—to women's tennis tournaments and other sporting events. Beer companies do the same thing, sponsoring auto racing teams and races, swimming meets, jazz and blues concerts and festivals, and other events.

Sponsorships are like celebrity product endorsements: not the real world. Do the famous people who promote sports shoes or soft drinks on TV use them? Maybe, maybe not; they get paid to deliver the message, not to use the product. Do the tennis stars who play in cigarette-sponsored tournaments smoke that brand? They probably don't smoke at all. Would an Indy race driver sponsored by a beer company guzzle down two or three brews before the call for the contestants to start their engines? Not likely!

What is the *real* reason for the roaring billboards, the easy-to-read banners, and the sponsorship? It is for name exposure, whether or not the brands can be legally advertised. It is for good old "brand awareness."

How to play that game: Enjoy the event. Ignore the sponsor.

Does Liquor Advertising Pay?

Just as smoking has an appeal because it's illegal for those under 18, drinking may attract people your age because it's illegal until you turn 21. And people your age *do* drink!

Surveys show that about 60 percent of high school seniors and 76 percent of college students aged 18 to 22 drink alcohol at least once a month. In a 1992 survey, 30 percent of high school seniors said they had taken five or more drinks in a row during the previous two weeks. The percentage of students who said getting drunk was "very important" or "somewhat important" was two to three times as high in 1989 as in 1977.

The alcohol industry recently fought hard against health warnings in ads, and won. The Federal Trade Commission did not accept legislators' arguments that advertising encouraged drinking. But Rep. Joseph P. Kennedy, Jr., cosponsor of the legislation, said, "Beer ads educate Americans, particularly younger Americans, that

40 taking a drink is needed in order to win that race, or make it down the ski slope, or land that account, or score with that new girl or guy."

One Speaker's Response

Not long ago, Harlan Ellison, a writer and TV commercial actor, freaked out a meeting of California advertising people. Ellison told them: "Your children use drugs, and you told them to do it....You've been pushing chemicals on TV for years: 'Can't sleep? Take a drug. Not happy? Take a drug.' ...Where in the world did people get the idea that it's smart to get in a car and go fast? To get in a 4-by-4 and tear up virgin land? You told them to do it....You rule the country. We have the reins to the most powerful medium in the world—television..."

Is Mr. Ellison right? Think about it as you watch ads on TV, or read ad messages. Ask yourself, *"Do I really need or want this?"* and *"Do I really believe this, or want to do this?"* In the case of alcohol and tobacco, doing what the sponsors want could get you into trouble.

CHAPTER 5

How Do Entertainment and News Persuade?

*D*o you pay attention to media messages? Surveys say you do. Young people aged 12 to 17 listen to radio an average of 2.5 hours a day. Seven out of ten of you watch television three hours a day.

The media have helped some entertainers become so popular that we know almost everything they do. Sports figures too have become famous because we "know" them through the media. Their doings are often pumped up with publicity that they pay for. It all helps sell movies, videos, concert tickets, CDs, and tapes.

Because the media follow the lives of famous people, we know the good and bad things they do.

42

The bad stuff can include doing drugs and abusing alcohol. Some entertainers recovering from drug-and-alcohol problems are talking about their experiences.

Five Sad Cases

Many rock musicians in the 1960s and 1970s were active on the drug scene. They praised drug-taking in songs and used drugs themselves. The message: "It's okay. Do your thing. If it includes drugs, fine."

What happened was not so fine.

Some rock musicians burned out from too much touring and too many drugs. Two of the best-known, guitarist Jimi Hendrix and singer Janis Joplin, died from drug overuse. In 1977, Elvis Presley, "The King," died of a heart attack, the result of addiction to prescription drugs.

Here were three of the most popular music stars of their day. They had it all— talent, money, fame. But they couldn't live without drugs. And they didn't live long *with* drugs!

Other famous entertainers who died too young because of drug problems were Marilyn Monroe and Judy Garland.

But these people "live on," mostly through the media. Every August, thousands of Elvis fans flock to his gravesite at

Elvis Presley's death in 1977 was caused by an addiction to
prescription drugs.

44 Graceland in Memphis. Would they go if their visits were not reported as news? Or do they make news because they visit the grave? Either way, this news sells more Elvis records, tapes, posters, and statues.

The glorification often mentions the way the person died, but somehow it makes the drug use seem OK. Now, Marilyn will always be beautiful. Elvis will always be sexy and powerful. Janis will always wow us with her voice. Jimi's on-stage energy will always be with us. The media make them legends. Legends are good for business. But all these people died before their time! If the media are playing deadly games with us, they are games we seem to welcome.

The Beat Goes On!

Entertainment has not changed much from the 1960s and 1970s. In *American Health* magazine, the American Medical Association wrote, "The messages portrayed by certain types of rock music may present a real threat to the physical health and emotional well-being of especially vulnerable children and adolescents." Among the hazardous rap and heavy-metal themes mentioned were drug-and-alcohol abuse, satanism, and suicide.

Much early rock and roll is still popular. **45** Many songs relate, or glorify, drug use. Drugs are mentioned in Keith Richards's "My Generation" and "The Kids Are Alright," Lou Reed's "Heroin," the Rolling Stones's hit "Monkey Man," a song by Steely Dan about "...the fine Colombian [cocaine]...," and songs by U2 from the recent movie "Bright Lights, Big City." The Black Crowes's music video "She Talks to Angels," is filled with drug references. Country singer George Thorogood's "I Drink Alone" and Jimmy Buffet's hit "Margaritaville" don't praise liquor, but they don't slam it, either. The Rastafarians of Jamaica are believers in marijuana, and much reggae music is about using pot. Even perfumes get into the act, with names like "Opium" and "Obsession."

This is a free country, and entertainment and the media are tied closely together. That makes it hard to limit what entertainers—and advertisers—say and do.

What About Drugs and the News?

The drug scene doesn't make the news too much. When it does, the stories are often about the failure of drug programs and enforcement steps. You'll see TV news stories and read headlines like these:

46

MARIJUANA GROWERS GO UNDER-
GROUND

WAR ON DRUGS LOST IN CLINICS:
THEY REAP FUNDS AS FAILURE
GROWS

SKIES ALL TOO FRIENDLY FOR DRUG
SMUGGLERS

Since the news part of the media re-
ports things as they are, the fact that the
war on drugs is only somewhat successful
is what you hear and read.

When the media report news, rarely are
a celebrity's drug use or alcohol problems
mentioned. The news media seldom talk
about what they can't prove. But tabloid
papers—more entertainment than news—
often pick up on problems. Celebrities
often sue these papers for big bucks for
printing lies—and sometimes they collect!

How do you handle all this? Go ahead,
pick your entertainment and watch the
news. But just as you should not be led by
advertisers, don't be led by everything you
hear and see in the news and entertainment media. Take a lesson from the 1960s:
Tune out, turn off—but this time only in a
positive way.

CHAPTER 6

How Do the Media Attack the Problem?

Conchita and Ramon walked home from high school together. They let themselves into the apartment and headed for the kitchen. Over snacks, they shared the morning newspaper. Ramon read the sports pages.

"No way! It can't be true," Ramon said. "Lyle Alzado's dead!"

"Who?"

"Football player. L.A. Raiders?"

"Oh, now I remember. Big, dark-haired guy."

"That's him."

"Wow! What did he die of?"

"I don't believe it," Ramon said. "It says he died of a kind of brain cancer. He

47

48 | *couldn't be operated on. And get this—he was using steroids for years, and he said before he died that he thought they caused the cancer."*

Brother and sister sat in silence.

How strange! Just yesterday, kids at school had been talking about the bulk-up and extra power you could get from using steroids. Ramon thought they might help his weightlifting. His friend Al said he could get some. But now? No way!

Media Reporting—Key to Antidrug Messages

Lyle Alzado's death was widely covered in the media. It sent a message. So did the 1992 death of one of the Marlboro Men. "Cigarettes will kill you," the commercial actor and model said. After crusading against smoking for two years, he died of lung cancer at age 51.

The media carry antidrug messages mostly as news. Since celebrities are newsmakers, much of it is about them:

- The Betty Ford Clinic was started by the wife of former U.S. president Gerald R. Ford. Years ago, Mrs. Ford admitted she was an alcoholic. Many famous people have gone to the clinic for help with their addictions.

Many celebrities help with antismoking campaigns. Here, singer Frankie Valli and actress Tina Louise crush a giant cigarette box.

50

- Movie star Drew Barrymore started drinking at age nine. She did drugs. Now she is clean and has written a book about her experiences.
- Many rock musicians and composers have gotten out of the drug scene, and talked about it. Elvis Costello said he was "just going to be a dead boy" if he didn't stop. Keith Richards admitted taking drugs and said "they never made anybody a better musician or better [song]writer." Pete Townshend said that in his "honeymoon period with heroin," he "wrote nothing and did nothing." And rock's Henry Rollins is absolutely against any kind of drug use.
- Aerosmith is one of several rock bands that have traded drugs and alcohol for health foods and sparkling water. Steven Tyler says, "I almost died" of drugs.
- Arnold Schwarzenegger, who used steroids as a bodybuilding competitor, now says he "doesn't believe in the usage of drugs in any sport."
- The soft rappers Kid N Play made a hip-hop comedy movie, "Class Act." Its antidrug message comes through loud and clear.

How the Media Fight Legal Drugs

One way the media fight alcohol and tobacco is straight news reporting. In Chicago, inner-city church members and the surgeon general marched to protest cigarette and liquor billboards too close to schools and too many in their neighborhoods. The media reported it. Similar marches occurred in New York, Baltimore, Dallas, and Detroit. Activists painted offensive billboards white. Some billboard companies did nothing; others agreed to replace cigarette and liquor signs with public-service announcements. Some advertisers stopped buying billboards in poor neighborhoods.

Joseph W. Cherner, who once worked on Wall Street, now is in the news. He spends his time and $100,000 of his own money each year fighting tobacco ads in New York. He started an antismoking contest that brought in 107,000 posters from students. He helped bring about a ban on tobacco ads in New York buses and subways. He has criticized the Tobacco Institute's "Helping Youth Say No" program because it never mentions cancer. It also sends the message that kids should not smoke because it's an adult thing to do. "That's exactly why kids start to

Young people sometimes want to experiment with smoking or drinking because it may look like fun in commercials.

smoke—because they want to be like adults," Cherner said in a recent newspaper interview.

The media also carry humorous antismoking comments. Garry Trudeau's daily comic strip "Doonesbury" uses Mr. Butts, a talking cigarette, to poke fun at the reasons for smoking. In a "Far Side" cartoon, the artist Gary Larson showed three trucks carrying advertising signs. One sign read, "Acme Guns—Goodbye, World!" The second was an ad for "Al's Hanging Ropes—The Best Way to Stretch Your Neck." The third truck pictured Joe Camel with a sly smile, holding out a pack of cigarettes.

Editorial cartoonists also make their points by poking fun. In one cartoon, Joe Camel is shown surrounded by young smokers, with the legend SMOOTH MARKETING over his head in big letters. This is a takeoff on Camels' SMOOTH CHARACTER theme. Another comments on the near-equal recognition of Mickey Mouse and the Marlboro Man by small children. It shows Mickey on horseback with the legend, "Marlboro Mouse." A third shows a childish-looking poster of tiny children talking to Santa Claus: "If you don't smoke our brand, Santa won't bring you any presents." Beside it, a cigarette company spokesman says, "It is *not* aimed at children!"

Antidrinking news stories, many involving groups like MADD (Mothers Against Drunk Driving) and SADD (Students Against Driving Drunk), appear often in newspapers and on TV news. And every antismoking, antidrinking, or antidrug protest is reported in the media.

Paid Messages Fight Drugs, Too

Although it comes nowhere near the money spent to advertise liquor and tobacco, antidrug activity and advertising are getting the message across:

54

- The U.S. government spends $250 million a year on drug prevention. Private funds for substance-abuse programs top $25 million a year.
- Celebrities are fighting against drugs: Nancy Reagan (who started the "Just Say No" program), the Rev. Jesse Jackson, Ben Vereen, and Michael Jordan.
- Since 1985, TV networks have given more than $275 million worth of time to antidrug ads.
- Orlando Woolridge of the L.A. Lakers and rap star Deezer D have made TV ads for a $26.8 million antismoking campaign.
- The "This Is Your Brain on Drugs" campaign with its fried-egg picture has changed attitudes toward hard drugs, according to surveys.
- Four out of five safe-drinking messages are actually paid for by beer companies. Brewers have voluntarily given more than $200 million to alcohol-abuse campaigns.
- "Alcohol, Drinking, Driving and You" (ADDY) is a 10-year-old safety program supported by Coors and other beer-makers.
- MTV has launched RAD, Rockers Against Drugs, with Jon Bon Jovi.

Working to keep your body healthy and fit can be very
rewarding.

Think Through the Confusion

The media carry confusing messages about the way we do things. For instance:

Tobacco kills 434,000 people a year, but the government spends less than $20 million a year on antismoking efforts, while tobacco companies spend $3.27 billion a year on ads and promotion. What is more, the U.S. government supports the tobacco industry in many ways. Legislation permits cigarette companies to buy surplus tobacco at bargain prices while supporting tobacco farmers and keeping them from losing money. The government also pressures Asian countries to allow the sale of American-made cigarettes.

Illegal drugs kill 7,000 people a year—1/62nd the number killed by tobacco—but the government spends more than $11 billion a year fighting illegal drugs.

While the Beer Institute gives money to 75 abuse-prevention programs, the **liquor industry** spends $2 billion a year on advertising. More than 18 million adults and several million teenagers have serious problems with alcohol. Over 100,000 deaths and 540,000 injuries a year are alcohol-related. Yet the U.S. government does not include alcohol in its war on drugs.

CHAPTER 7

Whose Life Is It, Anyway?

Life may be tough for you. (It is for most people.) But if drugs—legal or illegal—are a part of your life, or threaten to be, remember: it's *your* life, *your* body, and *your* brain that are on the line. If you want to keep clean, think about these suggestions:

- Take a good, hard, grown-up look at ads and entertainment. Don't believe everything you see, hear, or read.
- Remember to ask yourself, "Do I really need this?" "Do I really want to do this?"
- Pick your friends—don't wait for them to pick you.
- Start your own group, with people who see things your way. Remember the old saying, "To have a friend, be one."

57

Question what you hear and what you read. Develop your own
opinions and ideas.

- If you're tempted to try things you shouldn't, find an adult you trust to talk to: a parent, a relative, a teacher, a minister, or counselor.
- Seek positive approaches with your family if they are part of the problem.
- Find things to do that you enjoy. You may be able to help others, too.
- Study hard at school. It will pay off later.
- Remember, *it's your life*—the only one you have. Don't let drugs mess it up.

Glossary
Explaining New Words

acid Slang for LSD, a manufactured hallucinogen.

addiction Constant need to use a drug no matter what happens as a result.

advertisement Paid message that promotes a product or service.

alcoholism Addiction to the ethyl alcohol in beer, wine, and liquor.

amphetamines Drugs that speed up the central nervous system; also called **pep pills** and **uppers**.

angel dust Slang for PCP, a manufactured hallucinogen.

barbiturates Drugs that slow down or depress the central nervous system; also called **downers**.

caffeine Mild stimulant found in coffee, tea, and cola drinks.

chemical dependence Constant need to use a drug no matter what the result.

cocaine Powerful stimulant made from coca plant leaves.

controlled substance Any drug or chemical legally available only under special circumstances.

60

crack Most addictive form of cocaine.

crash, low The sickness and depression that follow a drug high.

denial Refusal to admit that you have a drug problem.

gateway drug Drug that leads to the use of more harmful drugs.

hallucinogen Drug that makes you see things that aren't there, or *hallucinate*.

hangover The aftereffect of overdrinking.

heroin Narcotic made from morphine.

high The temporary feeling of pleasure or strength induced by drugs.

hooked Dependent on drugs; addicted.

narcotic Painkiller or drug made from poppies, such as opium, morphine, and heroin.

shooting up Taking drugs by injection.

snorting Inhaling a drug.

steroids Controlled substances used illegally for building body mass and muscle bulk, and for increasing athletic speed.

stimulant Substance that speeds up your brain and makes you more alert.

tolerance The need to take more and more drugs to get the same effect.

withdrawal symptoms The illness, depression, and hallucinations that can last for days or weeks when getting off drugs, or when drugs are not available.

Help List

National Council on Alcoholism
1-800-622-2255

Alcoholics Anonymous
1-800-662-HELP

Drug and Alcohol Hotline
1-800-252-6465

Narcotics Anonymous
World Service Office
16155 Wyandotte St.
Van Nuys, CA 91406

Toughlove
P.O. Box 1069
Doylestown, PA. 18901

**National Federation of Parents for
  Drug-Free Youth**
1-800-554-KIDS

American Council for Drug Education
204 Monroe Street
Rockville, MD 20850
(301) 294-0600

For Further Reading

Berger, Gilda. *Making Up Your Mind About Drugs*. New York: Lodestar Books, 1988.

Hurwitz, Sue, and Shniderman, Nancy. *Drugs and Your Friends*, rev. ed. New York: Drug Abuse Prevention Library, Rosen Publishing Group, 1993.

McFarland, Rhoda. *Drugs and Your Parents*, rev. ed. New York: Drug Abuse Prevention Library, Rosen Publishing Group, 1993.

Perry, Robert. *Focus on Nicotine and Caffeine: A Drug Alert Book*. New York: Twenty-First Century Books, 1990.

Salak, John. *Drugs in Society*. New York: Twenty-First Century Books, 1993.

Schulman, Jeffrey. *Focus on Cocaine and Crack: A Drug Alert Book*. New York: Twenty-First Century Books, 1990.

Index

About the Authors
Richard S. Lee has an AB degree in English from The College of William and Mary. He is a career advertising writer and free-lance author. Mary Price Lee holds a BA in English and an MS in education from the University of Pennsylvania. She is a former educator, now a free-lance writer.

Photo Credits
Cover: Stuart Rabinowitz.
Page 20: Barbara Kirk; page 37: © Orlando Sentinel/Gamma-Liaison; page 43: Liaison Agency; page 49: Wide World Photos; all other photos: Stuart Rabinowitz.

Design & Production: Blackbirch Graphics, Inc.